The Enshrouded
An Overwhelmed Heart

B. A. Cooper

B. A. Cooper

In Memory of Matthew Cooper

World War II

'The Germans are coming,'

A little boy said,

Bullets flying, people dying,

Oh what a horrible time!

'The Spitfires are coming,'

A little boy said,

Bombs are dropping, things are popping

Oh what a horrible time!

'The British are coming,'

A little boy said,

To fight off the Germans, to kill them all dead

Oh what a horrible time!

'The war is over,'

A little boy said,

As he turned to his mother and she said,

'I know, now boy, it's time for bed.'

Contents

PAIN

Introduction

Within this book you will find the crying desires of my heart and the screaming thoughts of my mind. This is not a book to tell you how you must process any pain you face nor is it a book to tell you these are the only feelings you must have. Actually, the opposite is true. The thing about feelings is there are so many of them and every person will have such different approaches to universal themes. I write about love, pain and God - so you may find the words written in this book recognizable and comforting or you may feel like you're looking into a 16-year-old boy's life, which in fact you are.

The 3 main themes of this book are love, pain, and God - these have been the strongest themes throughout my life, so far. The common truth among these themes is that they all have brought positive and negative changes to my life. In my life I have felt so many different emotions from a young age. Due to my life experiences, I feel these emotions sometimes appear stronger than others of my generation, just as some waves crash stronger in the sea than others do. Yet, I also accept that I cannot see into other people's minds, so who knows the amount of emotion everyone feels. If you are like me, overwhelmed, sensitive and an all-feeling person, you will relate to how this can be hard to deal with. Therefore, within this book, I have carefully explored the waves of the sea that crash greater against the seashore of my head, then use them as an escape, and even release some of these deep thoughts. To enable you to recognize these thoughts and find comfort in knowing you are not alone, I can assure you that, even if you don't feel such emotions as strongly as I might, you will still feel them. These are some of the most important feelings in a person's life for shaping them and finding where they stand in the dizzy haze that is this world.

Love – love is everything and everywhere, it can break you down to dirt or build you up to feel like gold. Without love what do you have?

Pain – pain is also everywhere, and it can go hand in hand with love, but pain is not always bad. Pain is necessary to truly appreciate happiness and it is essential to truly love. If you can love someone, not just in the happy times when they make you feel infinite, but also when you fight and there is pain – then that is actual love.

God – God works through all these and every theme. In love - well God is love, there is no greater love than the love of God. The reason we love is because God loved us first (1 John 4:19). In pain God is always with us. He is there in the lowest moments of my life. The feeling of peace in a time of pain, is only the Lord. Even in the unbearable moments of our lives, there is no greater pain than the pain Jesus experienced on the cross, dying for our sin.

These 3 themes are deeper expressed within my life story which I have stated in my testimony (Pg11) and of course in my poems.

My poetry is not written in the style of modern poetry; I have always enjoyed older poets and their style of writing. My poems may be regarded as modern poems in the sense that they have been written in the 21st century but other than that, they are not modern. I write in an older sense of the word poetry. One or two are written in free verse, but the majority are sonnets, rhyming poetry and narrative poetry. This may be quite unusual for a younger person in this modern era to write in such an old-fashioned way, but I feel this form is best suited for the topics I'm dealing with. Modern poetry is very different, and although (I feel) it may give more freedom without the need for rhythm or structure, I do not feel as able to display such deep thinking and deep emotions in this way. Older words describe what I feel so much better, so occasionally I have used older words to help truly depict the feeling that I'm trying to capture. However, I have respect for everyone's opinion on this matter. I write in the style of my favourite poets such as William Shakespeare and Robert Burns. I will speak more about their inspiration on the pages to come and reference my favourite poets (on page 108) in case you are looking for a recommendation.

Testimony

These are the words which I spoke on the 16th May 2021, the day I got baptized in Craigavon Baptist Church in Northern Ireland:

Hello everyone, my name is Ben Cooper for all the people who don't know me. I grew up in Ballygawley, but Craigavon has always really been a part of me since I took my first breath in Craigavon Hospital. I grew up in a Christian family which I am extremely thankful for.

One night when I was about six years old, I remember going to bed, my mind full. My mum came to settle me, and I asked her if my brother Peter was saved and then asked the same about Adam and Matthew and dad too and then I asked how to become saved. That night I prayed to God for him to come into my life.

Even at that age I saw something my family had that I wanted, and it was Jesus. So years went by and I can't lie I was doubtful at points and prayed for God to come into my life a couple more times. This was mainly because of a fear of death and even today I struggle with that. The years kept going on and I went to youth clubs and church and holiday Bible clubs. Everyone I knew did the same and went to the same things and were Christians but then at the age of seven my faith was truly tested.

My eldest brother Matthew passed away and this was an incredible shock to my perfect bubble idea of Christianity. After that I felt a lot of anger towards God, and I blamed God for everything. I remember praying every night for God to bring him back and it never happened. That hurt, and the fact that in the Bible there are lots of stories of healing and miracles. So, I stopped praying and reading my Bible and even me and my family didn't really know how we would get better and rejoin society again. Then as months passed it got easier, slowly. The fact that life became bearable is partly due to a couple of families, especially one family who were extremely kind to me. There were many others who really helped me, and my family and I owe them all a lot.

The main person who got us through that time though is God. Even though I had turned my back on him he didn't turn his back to me, and he helped me and my family and even though we weren't strong enough to pray. The people who prayed for us helped immensely and really showed the power of God. As I saw this, I started praying more again because I needed God and still do.

So, after this - after all that pain- I still can proudly say I believe in God and God doesn't take people away. He was the Person who put Matthew in my life in the first place which I praise Him for every day. God has blessed me so much with great Christian friends and when my church was too painful to go to, we came here, and I can firmly say that I haven't met any people nicer than the people at Craigavon Baptist Church. Over the past years I have seen the love of these people and power of God working in this church.

Another massive part of my Christian journey was CEF camp where I felt God's love the most. I remember coming home from camp and just breaking down into tears because I had to leave and how great the week had been. Another reason I enjoyed it so much is because I met two of my friends there who are still my friends today and will always be. They have helped me a grow a lot as a Christian and having them there also is something I'm very thankful for.

Years passed and I was in second year at Aughnacloy College is when I started to properly process the death of Matthew and it was a bad couple of months. This meant I took a lot of time off school. But God was still with me and with help I got better again. Those were bad times, tough times but the fact that my family and I got through is one of the reasons why I have no doubts there is a God in heaven. I have grown in Christ, and I understand the Bible more and even understand the glory and goodness of God better. The main thing is I've grown in my faith and love for God

So, from second year to now I wouldn't say it's been easy, but it has been a lot easier and even in the past year I've felt the help and presence of God. I want to show publicly that I am a Christian and that I believe in God, and I will follow him my whole life till I see Him and Matthew in heaven. And what a glorious day it will be, and I hope you know Jesus personally as your Savior, so you will be there too.

About Author

I started writing poetry back in November 2021 when I picked up a book called 'The Songs of Robert Burns' which I bought when I went to Scotland with my family. I still remember my grandfather reading a poem from it called 'Scots Wha Hae' in his best Scottish accent. When I picked up this book, I remembered back to such a perfect time and the joy it had once given me as I lay listening to my grandfather, which in fact is one of the earliest memories I have (since I have forgotten a lot). This perfect memory led me to pick up the book again. I started to love the poems that Robert Burns wrote. As I read them – highlighting nearly every page - I was completely inspired, so I started writing myself. Poetry is such a powerful outlet as I can take all the thoughts, feelings and words in my head and organize them on a page which is such a cathartic experience.

I have loved music from a young age and as a boy with many dreams in my life I always wanted to become a musician. I have always been quite good at coming up with the lyrics of songs but then my musical inability created a lot of problems; I could never put a tune to the lyrics. Poetry is perfect for me, because I can just write and don't have to do the complicated part that music brings.

It would completely unfair not to mention my Speech and Drama teacher too. She introduced me to so much poetry as well as introducing me to William Shakespeare and the Shakespearean sonnets. As you will see in this book several of my poems were greatly inspired by William Shakespeare and although I might not have loved learning them at the time, I am incredibly thankful the role that she played.

The most recent thing that sold me completely on poetry was surprisingly not a person or a book, it was a movie called 'Dead Poetry Society' directed by Peter Weir. This movie reveals such painful beauty that it leaves you lying in a melancholy wonderland. Within this movie there is one main poem by Walt Whitman called 'Oh Captain! My Captain!' (Which I urge you to read). This poem is read repeatedly throughout the movie and ends beautifully with that reoccurring title and first line. After watching the movie I read this poem and fell in love with how beautiful it was. From there I read more poems by Walt Whitman. Through him I found other similar poets, fell down the rabbit hole that is equally beautiful and tragic until now I have a whole collection of poetry books that make me want to write every time I read them.

Reason For Publishing

If you are reading this book, it means I am officially an author and a poet which brings me such joy to think about. On this day a dream has been accomplished, and I thank you greatly for buying my first book!

I have written this book not to become well known or famous, no not at all. I wrote this because I feel that my poetry, as much as it helped me, could help others. I want to inspire young minds of this generation to just let their feelings and emotions out and portray moments in their life through an art form, maybe with a simple structure and rhythm.

I really hope that after reading this book, you will go on to read more poetry or even have a go a writing for yourself. Just take a simple emotion or something you're interested in and write about it. It is a fantastic way to let out feelings that can easily get a hold of you and you never know the beauty that you could create.

-    *B. A. Cooper*

B. A. Cooper

<u>LOVE</u>

Sonnet 1 - The Warmth Of 1000 Suns

Her eyes are like a sunset on a soft mountain peak.

Her lips like the campfire warming up the woods.

Nothing grasps my attention more than the words of which she speaks,

And with a simple smile she orients my moods.

Thy art shy tho' her smile says more than 1000 words   5.

Her skin tis' soft and white like lilies.

Her name is like the melody sung in the morn' by the birds.

Her touch is like a snowflake delicately floating down.

Her words overflow like morning dew off a petal.

Her hair is as smooth as a lake in the dead of night.   10.

Now that I've seen her face there is no one I'd rather settle,

She is more pure, far rarer, and holds greater value than gold.

    When she says my name, I feel the warmth of 1000 suns,

    She is my world, my everything, she is the one.

Sonnet 3 - When I Think of My Luv'

When I think of my luv I think of the trees,

A world out there waiting to be seen.

When I think of my luv I think of the bees,

To see their complexity, pureness and keen.

When I think of my luv I think of the ocean,   5.

A calm presence and a calming motion.

When I think of my luv I think of a potion,

One that can make me feel every emotion.

When I think of my luv I think of the sun,

So many planets rotating round the brightest one.   10.

When I think of my luv I think of a run,

And the feeling of such satisfaction when it is done.

  As long as the grass grows and sky is blue,

  As long I shall love and forever cherish you.

Sonnet 6 - When I Gaze Upon Her Eyes

When I gaze upon her eyes

I see that God is looking back,

And by heaven she is wise

No such spirituality does she lack.

When my hand grazes upon her hair   5.

And I see how she is made,

The beautiful hand of God declares

She is made by God and in God is not afraid.

When I look upon her sunset lips,

With power to create or kill   10.

Like a rose has thorns and sharp tips,

But she chooses to do the Lord's will.

    It is not a kiss but what she says that pleases me more,

    "My Saviour, my God, I sing praise to the one whom I adore".

Flower In the Night

My flower awakens in the darkness of the night,

The stars are her comforter, she has no fright,

The moon is her guide, her lover, her source of light,

There is such beauty with my flower in the night.

My flower in the night was lost but now found,

As it grows oh so tall, my flower looks around,

And sees the moon and the stars which astound,

There is such beauty with my flower in the night.

My flower in the night cries out for me,

As she is so adoring and loves no other bee,

If you look around there isn't more beauty to see

Than the great beauty of my flower in the night.

B. A. Cooper

The Rocks and Strange Clocks

The trees and the woods

Look down with solitude,

They cry out with pain

Hidden under night's hood.

The woods and the caves

With such secret faces,

Echo sounds from the grave

Hidden under these places.

The caves and the rocks

Each uniquely made,

Speak of a different clock

Hidden under the shade.

The rocks and strange clocks

Which create different times,

When time finally unlocks

The woods and the sky aligns.

B. A. Cooper

Did I Not Ever Feel Happiness Til' Today?

Did I not ever feel happiness til' today

Or ever feel such peace rush over me?

I swear I never have felt this way

Until you opened my eyes to see.

Was it happiness or you?

But maybe you are the same,

But if this statement is true

Then let me draw closer to thy name.

People look for happiness all around

But yet it came to me,

And this happiness walks and sounds

It was she who set me free.

Beauty All-Around

Why is the garden so green?

Is this the beauty I have not yet seen?

Why is the sky so blue?

Is this a colour that I have always knew?

Why are the trees so dark?

Have I ever seen brighter bark?

Why are the faces so blue?

Is this how I look to others too?

Why in this world with such beauty

Is everyone around it so moody?

Stop and look and wait and see

The beauty that's around you and me.

Our Love Disobeys Time

Life is quick, life is fast,

Life is big, life is vast,

Life is here, life has past,

This day may be the last.

Love is good, love is slow,

Only love cares, our love grows,

Our love was found long ago.

A waste it would be to let it go.

Life with you is the best,

I look at you and I feel blessed.

In you I find love, in you I find rest.

My love for you is uneasily expressed.

Heaven's Descent

Thy fair beauty,

She is the depiction of love,

As she appears from above,

Like that of a dove.

Thy fair beauty,

She is love's aching cheer,

As she suddenly appears,

In the spotlight of a deer.

Thy fair beauty,

She is love's true touch,

To hold her hand is too much,

To hold her is to love her as such.

B. A. Cooper

Thy fair beauty,

She is home's sweet scent,

But tis' not where she is meant,

Because she an angel of heaven's descent.

Beauty Unseen

I feel the wind, I see the trees,

I feel as though I'm finally free.

I see pastels of blue, brown, and green

I see the place where I'm meant to be.

I feel the sun, I see the sky,

I feel as though I'm finally alive,

I see colours of blue, like that of an eye

I see the place where my darling dos' lie.

I feel the love, I see the world,

I feel her glance and love unfurled,

I see colours of pale, like that of soft snow

I see her now like I knew her long ago.

The Weather

For the soft snowflake drops

Are her tears of laughter,

These tears of such are the beautifulness of her.

For the heavy raindrops

Are her tears of sadness,

These tears of such are the essence of mist.

For the hurtful hailstones

Are her tears of anger,

These tears of such are the colour of amber.

And for the bright blissful sun

Is the beauty which she beholds,

And this beauty which moulds into the colour of pure gold.

O' My Heart Is Full

I think of my love

Every day and night,

She flies like a dove,

All I see is beautiful white.

O' my heart is full.

I dream of my love

Every night I see,

She flies like a dove,

But does she dream of me?

O' my heart is full.

I vision my love

More than I should,

B. A. Cooper

She flies away like a dove,

If I could catch her I would.

O' my heart is full.

The Age of Love

May the trees wither,

And no more growth on the vine,

And let clouds come full and empty

But only love stands time.

May the crops die out,

And no more grapes for wine,

And let buildings be blown away

But only love stands time.

May the people grow old,

And let that be a sign,

That only love doesn't falter

But only love stands time.

B. A. Cooper

To Freeze or Burn

Why must my tender heart burn,

While you live with such ease?

Why do you cast not a look?

My heart yearns for your please.

Why must you let me grow weary?

Bring me along like a dog on a lead,

And then leave me for dead.

Just let me know if you love me, I plead.

Toss me away like a rock in a cave,

Or draw nearer and admit your desire.

And if this love is true it will save,

For I cannot freeze while I'm warm by a fire.

Scars of Perfection

I am so broken

But then again so are you,

Will we be broken together?

Or will you make me new?

Notice the burns,

The scratches on my heart

Born out of love for you,

When we have been so far apart.

You are a mess

But that's the bit I love most,

The scars make you human

And in that you can boast

37

B. A. Cooper

No one loves you like me,

No one wants you like me,

Throughout all the pain

A beautiful woman is what I see.

Life Without You is Unnatural

How can a fish say goodbye to water?

How can a penguin say goodbye to snow?

To say goodbye to you,

Is like swimming against a river's flow.

How can the moon say goodbye to the stars?

How can the sun live without heat?

To say goodbye to you,

Is like a herbivore eating meat.

You are the light in the darkness,

You are the gleaming moon in my sky.

To say goodbye to you,

Would be worse than to die.

Modern Romance

There are movies of young and books of old,

And tales of love and tales untold.

But what fits in to this perfect mould?

Do not buy into the love that is sold.

Do not buy into the love that is sold,

For nothing but lies in these stories are told,

This love does not provide warmth in the cold.

Do not let these false ideas get a hold.

Do not let these false ideas get a hold,

Do not let relationships be a threshold,

To be a fool is to leave this love uncontrolled,

This love is like a worthless leaf painted gold.

The Words of Love

The words of love are quiet and still,

But in the deepest love are shrill.

Love can pierce your heart and burn your soul,

Love is an unachievable goal.

The words of love can be deceitful,

Soft harmonies, pretty people,

Your heart may let out longing's full cries,

Love is but a concoction of lies.

The words of love may be damaging,

Tis wild and rare and ravaging,

But true love is real, peaceful, stands tall -

And, in the end, true love conquers all.

Woman Of Thy Beauty

Woman of thy beauty,

With marble eyes and hair that shines,

And with her stunning body

Are any man's dreams, may they cross lines.

Woman of thy beauty,

With perfect skin and soft hair that's dim,

And a gold light from heaven.

Are any man's dreams when welcomed in.

Woman of thy beauty,

With fake smiles and judgmental eyes,

And with their boastful stories.

Are any man's dreams where horrors lie.

Woman of thy beauty,

With gravel eyes and hair of rags,

Seen through the eye of their heart.

No man's dreams for self-adored hags.

B. A. Cooper

She Is Beauty

For sweetness lies in her eyes

And beauty drips from her cheek,

That which lies in what she speaks

Can make the strongest man feel so weak.

I'm lost in space, in her face,

She is far purer than a crystal lake

And from her silky hair drips grace,

She is the main reason that I awake.

A Good Addiction

I did not have a type

Until today,

But now thy type is found

It's you, and not in any other way.

People seem to think

That green eyes are better blue,

Or ginger nicer brown,

But I think that thy best is you.

Why would one change

When thou already perfect?

You are my greatest weakness

And I your adoring addict.

B. A. Cooper

Wilt Not Thy Love Bring More Joy?

Wilt not thy love bring more joy,

Than that of a favourable flame?

Wilt not mere love bring more joy,

Than that of thy glory, riches, and fame?

Wilt not such love but only destroy?

Even if so, it would not be in vain.

Wilt not mere love bring more joy?

I cannot love but you - if so, then shame.

The Dream of a Boy

I dream of being a hero,

A great and noble king.

In reality, my chance is zero,

But who knows what luck shall bring?

I dream of being an artist,

A creative piece of mind.

It may be a very far-fetched wish,

But who knows the luck someone can find?

I dream of being a poet.

A romantic sort of guy,

My chance is low, and I know it,

But who knows what luck can buy?

I dream of being a husband

And a father to my child.

I see myself holding his tiny, small hand,

Is that really a dream too wild?

If I Was Like You

"If I was like you," the little boy said,

"Then I would be so tough and brave.

I would stay up and never go to bed,

Because no one would tell me how to behave."

"If I was like you," the little boy said,

"I would have big strong legs and arms,

And be filled with such cleverness in my head,

And I would save the world from harm."

"If I was like you," the little boy said,

"Then I would look so very good

And do big boy things instead,

Like watching TV and chopping firewood."

"If only you, were you," said the man to the boy,

"Then you would be the best of the best and give out so much joy,

But I'm afraid for now it's time to go to bed and get some rest.

But sleep well my beautiful son, for you are heaven blessed."

PAIN

B. A. Cooper

Sonnet 5 - How Can One Find Love?

With a world driven by sex,

How can one find love?

If no one feels no more,

How can one find love?

If love is based on image.   5.

How can one find love?

If the word has no meaning,

How can one find love?

This world is mean and cold,

How can one find love?   10.

And no one really wants,

How can one find love?

      The birds in the sky seem to still find love up above,

      Maybe it's our own fault that no one can find love.

Sonnet 7 - The Things You'll Miss

You left me when I was seven

Not on purpose of course,

And I know I'll see you in heaven,

But I can't leave you without some remorse.

You won't be there when I marry   5.

Or even when I drive,

So this burden that I carry,

I carry until the day I die.

I know that you are better

But what about me?   10.

Wish I could have gotten a letter,

Until then I'm broke internally.

    It's hard to process this time, your face I cannot see,

    But I'll take this price for that I know; I'll be with you for eternity.

B. A. Cooper

Driving In the Dark

Driving in dark

Without any light,

Is calming and peaceful

And quiets the night.

Driving in the dark

Under the streetlight,

Is strangely restful

As the cars are in full might.

Driving in the dark

I look up at the last second,

And work out what I see

As death slowly beckons.

Driving in the dark

We didn't see the car,

But the time slows down

Until we crash in full power.

Driving in the dark

In the middle of a crash,

Is calming and peaceful

Until there nothing but ash.

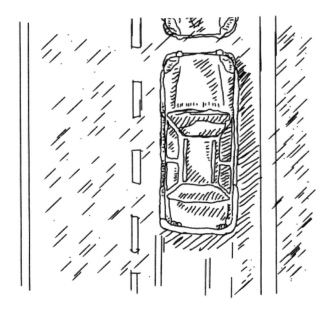

Time Thief

When time is gone and left,

And there is nothing to be done.

You think of time as theft,

Then you are the guilty one.

The Dark, Early Morn'

I remember the noise in the dark, early morn'

I wake and investigate this 2 o'clock laughter.

As soon as I'm up I'm greeted by my daddy, rather torn.

Tells me, "Go back to bed, it's nothing just us."

I plead with my father, "Let me come down",

I win and walk with excitement in every step.

I cracked open the door, but it's gone alown,

I am greeted by a policeman who says, "It's nothing just us."

I turn to my left and a horrifying sight to see,

I look from each face - all sparkly eyes and pale, damp cheeks.

It was my family hurdled together but not filled with glee.

I look toward my mummy, and she says, "It's nothing just us."

What I saw on that early morn, I wish to forget every day.

As I scan through the faces one more time with pain,

Then I look through the window and not more can I say.

But it wasn't nothing, it was 'us' never again.

The Closing Door

I never saw you smile like that before,

Well at least never with me.

They say in life when one door closes there is another door,

But you're that last one I could see.

Was I not good enough for you?

Because it feels so,

I just wish ahead of time you could have let me know.

That you would leave me feeling so low.

The Men of The Age

The men of the age

Are cowardly and unbrave.

They do not stand up for women and save

Instead, they make women of society slaves.

These men will never fill out their own graves.

The men of the age

Forever on the same page,

Do not help make life easier for the women and pave

The path for young men, instead they teach them to enslave.

These men will never fill out their own graves.

The men of the age

Who just sit and gaze,

And forget that their fathers' hands are still grazed

Not just to assault, disrespect and make object or slave

But so that they might just fill out their own graves.

Modern Words

With words of thy modern days,

How can one really speak passion?

Without those majestic ways,

Are such feelings now out of fashion?

With words of thy modern days,

How can any speak of pain?

Those who feel love's sharp rays,

Modern words cannot explain.

I Spoke to Your Love Yesterday

I spoke to your love yesterday,

It told me it is giving up.

Says it feels some other kind of way,

And that I'm just not enough.

I spoke to your feelings yesterday,

But they didn't speak to me.

Just stood like a wall in the way,

As it always seems to be.

I spoke to your desires yesterday,

But she didn't seem interested.

Like I was a cold, windy rain in May,

But there was a warmth more blessed.

If She Wanted To, She Would've

If she wanted to then she would've,

Is one of life's hard facts,

But she didn't even though she could've,

So, move on and forget her acts.

She's too nice to tell the truth,

That she wants nothing to do with you.

I've wondered throughout my youth,

Would it be better if she spoke what she knew?

If she had spoken what she knew,

I would have saved so much time,

One big blow to the heart

Instead of dying in each and every line.

Missing You

I think of you from time to time

Little moments that passed us by,

But I see you in these gentle rhymes

To say I don't miss you is such a lie.

Dementia

I see through her eyes there is nothing left,

She looks at me and sees a stranger,

As If her mind was stolen by theft

But she has no pain or no danger.

I see that she is lost in her head and confused,

She doesn't know what is going on,

At least she seems content, happy, amused

Even though we are lost, we are gone.

Such an illness belongs with the devil,

That which corrupts the mind,

Disappearing memories, curses the revel

She is in recursion, she is purblind.

Dead To Sin

Sadness overcomes me,

Love overwhelms me,

And fear overthrows me,

In such sin I am not free.

Sickness overcomes me,

Death overwhelms me,

And tiredness overthrows me,

In such sin I am not free.

Weakness overcomes me,

My life needs a revive,

And the hate overthrows me,

In such sin I am, but alive.

Living In Pain

Why is there pleasure in pain?

Why is the hurt nicer than anything spoken?

Maybe it's because to heal,

You must be already broken.

Throughout my entire life,

There has been one common theme

Happiness has come and left,

But the Pain has always been.

Why must I fall into the role,

Of a sad and messed up boy?

Is this just who I am,

Or in life will I find joy?

Why is there pleasure in hurt?

Why does the plunge burn more than the dive?

Why does happiness suddenly invert?

Why in feeling dead do I weirdly feel alive?

B. A. Cooper

I Am Nothing Like the Sun

Oh, how the sun shines so bright,

But I feel so dark.

Oh, how the sun shines so warm,

But I feel so cold.

Oh, how the sun shines with beauty,

But I feel so ugly.

Oh, how the sun is perfectly placed,

But I am not.

Insufficient Time

Life is increasing in fear and stress

And still people ask how I cope with such a mess.

And if poetry was time, then I'm running out of rhymes,

But I just need to remember to take one day at a time.

Life is the monster that's under the bed,

And by under the bed, I mean in the back of my head.

I fear the end of my life as I can hear each year chime,

But I just need to remember to take one day at a time.

Life is the wheel as it's consistently spinning,

I want and fear the day that the end is the beginning.

It's a short life to live or die in this life of mine,

But I just need to remember to take one day at a time.

B. A. Cooper

The Contrast of Life

There is pain in love, yet well I know

That there is more pain in loss,

But something due, that's greater too,

The pain of leaving someone's life.

There is hurt in love, yet well I know

That there is more hurt in loss,

But someone who, had hope in you

Walks out the door and leaves your life.

There is rage in love, yet well I know

That there is more rage in loss,

When the storms brew, and the sun moves

The world can feel dark in your life.

There are tears in love, yet well I know

That there are more tears in loss,

But something new, when tears are through

The dark clouds are leaving your life.

There is hope in love, yet well I know

That there is no more hope loss,

But randomly so, as people go

Can just walk straight into your life.

B. A. Cooper

In The Spring Will I Know you?

I am so empty,

I don't hear your voice in my dreams as much anymore –

When I do

I cry.

Even the happy memories of you are slowly

Falling away from me

Like the leaves in winter -

Am going to completely forget you?

I tell myself everyday just because you're dead

Doesn't mean you not my brother,

But you're starting to feel less and less true.

The fact is that all I have left of you is those leaves

But I'm unsure if they will grow back in Spring again.

GOD

B. A. Cooper

Sonnet 2 - Addiction

Wild is the monster that stalks me at night.

He sneaks into my room and stands with such might,

Providing fake comfort, saying he will make it alright.

I give in to his lies and feel nothing but poor.

The monster in my room tells me to hide,   5.

Tells me that there is no one in whom I can confide,

He rips open my chest and leaves nothing inside.

I feel like a rabbit in a trap of grandeur.

Great is my God who holds me vast,

Great is my God who forever will last.   10.

He holds my hand tight, till the monster has passed.

I do not give in and feel everything and more.

With the strengths of my Lord and his almighty roar,

I can fight off this monster, I can close over that door.

Sonnet 4 – To Live for God

Lord, I feel weak,

Lord, I can't keep going,

Like a broken beak

I'm fragile, can't speak.

Lord, I feel sick,   5.

Lord, I can't stand,

The sin is a kick

That's slowly killing me quick.

Lord, I feel needy,

How did you stay tame?   10.

When I feel all this pain

Lord, I cry out your name.

    Lord, lighten the load, brake open the reins,

    Lord to live for you and to die is gain.

Prayer 1 - Temptation

Lord, I'm not perfect,

Lord, I'm not right.

I know the way,

And I've had to fight

Between right or wrong,

In the darkest of nights.

I don't always win,

'Plead forgiveness', I write.

I have not always turned to you,

When sin is in sight,

But when I have,

I have felt your glorious light.

B. A. Cooper

There is pleasure in the serpent,

But sin is an agonizing bite.

I feel unclean, shameful agony, but

I will forever have faith in my Lord Jesus Christ.

Prayer 2 - Oh Leader, My Lord

Oh Leader, My Lord

How great is your power?

In you I find freedom,

In you I find more.

Oh Leader, My Lord

You hold me in storms,

In you I find peace,

In your arms I mourn.

Oh Leader, My Lord

Such pain that I feel,

In you I find rest,

Without you, can't deal.

B. A. Cooper

Oh Leader, My Lord

Have you left me alone?

Without you, no hope,

Without you, no home.

Oh Leader, My Lord

Even tho' I don't feel,

I will continue to worship,

For I know you are real.

Prayer 3 - Change My Heart

My heart is cold, Oh God,

What I desire is not of you.

Although I'm sinful and flawed,

Can you still love me too?

This world is cold, Oh Lord,

And filled with pain, I know,

I know what comes with the sword.

Heaven or hell's blow.

And as think of this sword.

Well, my heart is warming through,

I plead, I finally find my peace,

When I reach my home with you.

Castlerock

There is a place,

Where your feelings melt wi' the sun,

And in this case

This is the place where my heart is one.

There is a place,

Where the wind speaks encouragement,

And in this case

This is the place where my heart is meant.

There is a place,

Where the rocks echo words of peace,

And in this case

This is the place where my heart pains cease.

There is a place,

Where such beauty lies in the docks,

And in this case

With God, at the place of Castlerock.

B. A. Cooper

The Good Farmer

There is young fox in the grassy bay,

If he moves one step,

He will be turned into prey,

But if he stays still, he will be shot on this day,

How long can he live in this way?

There is a young fox in a trap he is stuck,

Howls o' this fox

Such is the pain, covered in muck.

He will die in the morning if he is in luck,

How long can he live in this way?

There is a young fox who is like you and me,

Stuck in one spot,

Even tho' he has places to be.

He is lost in the world, blinded, can't see,

But the good farmer comes to set the young fox free.

The World's Illustrator

I am no slave to any but God,

For a father's son can't have another father

Who has made and cared for thee.

So be it true for me and my brothers.

God is my king and for no other I bow,

For a king in this world knows no such power

Than the King who I serve, and I vow

He has made these kings just as he made the flowers.

So, tell me what other such God is greater,

Than the world's Author and Creator?

There is no man, no king, nor dictator,

Greater than the God who is the World's Illustrator.

Friend Or Foe?

Are thy shadows friend or foe?

Does thy darkness hide or show?

Is thy blackened, unbeatable though?

If it is my friend, will it let me go?

Are thy shadows all they seem?

Are thy shadows dark and mean?

And will this darkness be there for me?

Not when light is near or seen.

Thy shadows aren't friend nor foe,

What can make thy darkness go?

Only that of which pure light glows,

My lord, My Light will save me, I know.

B. A. Cooper

Death Is Just the Start

For death is not the end,

It is the start of days to spend

In heaven with family again,

No more suffering, no more pain.

For death is just the start,

When I receive my perfect heart,

When I touch upon the lion's mane

No more sinning, no more pain.

God's Warmth

In the sun I feel the Lord,

In all his beauty and might.

This magnifies His love

Through this glorious light.

In the rain I still feel God,

Although it's not as bright.

He is there in all seasons

And in that I can delight.

B. A. Cooper

Upon That Perfect Day

When heaven comes to knock on the door,

Then I should be so blessed,

And leave this sightless and aimless world

And be still in my Father's rest.

When heaven comes to knock on the door,

Like a fast-paced dancer,

As death comes quicker, so do the knocks

That loving knock I shall answer.

As I leave this sightless, aimless world,

The worries slip far away,

Like that of a strong breeze that took me

Upon that perfect day.

A CATHARSIS

A Catharsis

I write poetry within dark hours of the night,

When my feelings and thoughts come out.

Within these times, when feelings are in might

I leave my feelings on this paper.

I write poetry when on top of the mountain,   5.

When my thoughts are the same as the clouds.

And as these thoughts float down like a fountain

I leave my feelings on this paper.

I write poetry when I'm near to the seaside,

When the water laps against my feet.   10.

I think of times where I've laughed and cried,

I leave my feelings on this paper.

I write poetry when driving late in the car,

When I feel nothing but silence and peace,

Feelings at this time are strange and bizarre,   15.

I leave my feelings on this paper.

I write poetry when tragedy hits upon me,

Within pain, loss and love, or all of the above,

When my mind and my heart disagree

I leave my feelings on this paper.   20.

I write poetry when love has gone and left,

When she is more interested in others than me,

When she steals my heart in account of theft

I leave my feelings on this paper.

I write poetry when life has got me down,   25.

When I feel like no one cares and I am alone,

When feelings of guilt almost make me drown

I leave my feelings on this paper.

I write poetry when life feels like it's too much,

When the cycle of work feels like it won't end,   30.

When I can't see passed the rainy clouds as such

I leave my feelings on this paper.

I write poetry when giving praise to my Lord,

When I feel the Lord's glorious, shining light,

While I look to the day of judgment of the sword   35.

I leave my feelings on this paper.

I write poetry when dealing with such stress,

When life is overwhelming and too much,

And I feel like I'll never get out of such a mess

I leave my feelings on this paper. 40.

I write poetry when my heart is filled with desire,

And there are so many strong feelings of love,

When my mind is frozen and my heart's on fire

I leave my feelings on this paper.

I write poetry when I'm feeling inspired or not, 45.

When I'm full of ideas or got nothing left,

I still display these feelings with a rhyming plot

And leave my feelings on this paper.

B. A. Cooper

THE TWO WINDOWS

The Two Windows

I look inside an old, rusted house

I see not a human nor a mouse

But from upstairs I hear a beautiful sound

So, I search, and I search until it is found

I walk up the stairs and the sounds grew   5,

It sounds like my childhood or something I knew

The floorboards creek but I pay no attention

I just keep listening as the boards squeak with the tension

Getting closer to the top, the sound is overwhelming

But there's a new sound, another story it's telling   10.

This second sound, not as pretty as the first

Creates such a worry as I hear a mighty burst

Like a soldier in the way that I march up the stairs

I could feel every bone, every beat, and every hair

As I reach the top, I would never wish unseen   15.

 I saw two widows one dirty, one clean

One seemed older and one seemed pristine

And in each window, there was a different scene

The one on the right with flowers all round

Could be made out to be producing the nostalgic sound 20.

And through the glass I seen a golden city

We're everyone knew each other and there was no pity

And I stepped forward as I saw a lion stepped out

He carried such beauty and I felt I knew him without
doubt

I stood mesmerized by this amazing window   25.

The Enshrouded Desires of An Overwhelmed Heart

I felt a sharp, cold breath down below

As I slowly look down away from the lion
The shrieking came back

I suddenly turned to look to the one on the left
This had a vine of serpents; my heart left my chest   30.

With great fear I look through but saw nothing
So, I slowly took a step forward, the sound still coming

And until I was directly in front of the glass
The sound stopped, I felt relieved, it has passed

I saw a snake slithering right beside me until   35.
It climbed up the wall and lay on the window still

It went through the window into the darkness
I wanted to look away, but I couldn't, it was a strangeness

As I went to turn away a strange light appeared

Then as quickly as the light came so did the rush of fear 40.

The harder I look the bigger the light got

Like my eyes were in a trap, stuck and caught

As the light grew brighter so did my fear

Until the light turns off, but the fear didn't disappear

Then as sudden as the next a black dragon rose   45.

I shake in my one spot as the dragon grows

It lets it a roar so different to the lion's call

With a high-pitched sound that shakes all the walls

And the walls as they shook crumbled in fear

I shouted as I felt the dragon was getting near   50.

It was looking at me, directly in the eye

And I panicked as I thought I might die

Until the roar came back again

But not a roar that's filled with fear

I looked to the window on the right   55.

As just as I knew it was the lion's bright light

This light filled the room and forced the dragon back

And I start slowing stepping back as the floor started to crack

This blinding light is something I've never seen before

I finally turn around and run down the stairs and out   60.
the door

Every day I thought about this house

Even when I was old and had children and a spouse

But one day came sooner than I dreamed

I was near the end of my life as it seemed

So, I came back to the old, rusted house   **65.**

And it was silent, still wasn't a mouse

Walking up the stairs was harder than the last

I gripped tight to the handrail, and I heard that sound
from the past

After a long time, I reached the very top floor

I looked straight to the right as the sound grew more   **70.**

Without hesitation I walked straight through that glass

Into that golden city with the golden grass

And on that day when I went to Zion

I only remember life with me and the Lion.

Neologistics

of B. A. Cooper

<u>Vux</u> – *v-ux*

*A feeling that you are too busy to even be able to process your own thoughts. / "I have so many things to do, I feel so **vux**".*

<u>Drate</u> – *dr-ate*

*A drain of emotions from your head so your head feels virtually empty but so much so that it feels peaceful. / The feeling of **drate**.*

<u>Nicated</u> – *ni-kate-ed*

*A relationship of natural love that feels although it has always been there, and you can't remember a time when you didn't know and love them. / A **nicated** friendship.*

<u>Rost</u> – *rost*

*A type of love that is so strong that they could do anything, and you would still love them. / A **rostful** love.*

<u>Moraw</u> – *more-ah*

*The feeling that you are not good enough and everything you do makes people dislike you more. The harder you try the more that person hates you / The feeling of **moraw.***

<u>Paragrot</u> – *par-a-grot*

*The feeling that you will never find love, as hard as you try you will always not be good enough. / The feeling of **paragrot.***

<u>Randit</u> – *ran-dit*

*The inability to open up to people and tell them how you really feel. / "I feel so trapped I'm in a state of **randit**".*

<u>Dyrate</u> – *die-rate*

*When you reach a point of which you can't cope with the stress of life and are completely fed up, unmotivated and tired. / The point of **dyrate.***

<u>Alown</u> – *a-loun*

*A sudden drop in noise / the room went **alown**.*

Glossary

Word	Meaning
orient	*A change (in this case of emotions).*
Luv'	*Love*
tis'	*It is.*
Tho'	*Though*
cherish	*Protect and care for (someone) lovingly.*
solitude	*The state or situation of being alone.*
dos'	*Does.*
unfurled	*To be spread out.*
shrill	*High-pitched and piercing.*
beckon	*To summon.*
alown	*Quiet.*
revel	*Lively and noisy enjoyment.*
recursion	*The repeated application of a recursive procedure or definition. / Being in a loop.*
purblind	*Having impaired or defective vision; partially blind / slow or unable to understand.*
grandeur	*Splendour and impressiveness, especially of appearance or style.*
wi'	*With.*
Catharsis	*The process of releasing strong or repressed emotions.*
Neologistics	*The introduction or use of new words or new senses of existing words. / In this case the new words of B. A. Cooper*

Inspirational Poets

C.S. Lewis
Robert Burns
Seamus Heaney
William Shakespeare
Walt Whitman
Robert Frost
William Wordsworth
Emily Dickenson
Rudyard Kipling
William Ernest Henley
T. S. Elliot
Lord Byron

B. A. Cooper

FOR GOD

Printed in Great Britain
by Amazon

80137614R00068